REINVENTING THE GLOBE

For Maggie

and with warm thanks to James Brockway for his encouragement

Reinventing the Globe

MALCOLM BRADLEY

To Peter —

very best wishes

from

Malcolm

Sept. '06

ACKNOWLEDGEMENTS

Some poems in this collection have previously appeared in:
*Bulletin of the Welsh Academy, Coal City Review,
Envoi, The Frogmore Papers, Oasis, Poetry Wales, Seam,
Staple, Slipstream, Smiths Knoll, Tears in the Fence,
Thumbscrew, The Western Mail.*

'Origins' won first prize in the Gwyl Conwy Festival
Poetry Competition in 1995. 'The Voyage of Emma Darwin'
won first prize in the same competition in 1996.

The author wishes to thank the Arts Council of Wales for the financial
assistance that made it possible for him to complete this collection.

Published with the financial support of the Arts Council of Wales.

*

First published in the UK in 2000 by Flambard Press
Stable Cottage, East Fourstones, Hexham NE47 5DX

Typeset by Harry Novak
Cover design by Gainford Design Associates
Printed by Cromwell Press, Trowbridge, Wiltshire

A CIP catalogue record for this book
is available from the British Library.

ISBN 1 873226 38 1

© Malcolm Bradley 2000
All rights reserved

Flambard Press wishes to thank Northern Arts for its financial support.

CONTENTS

Origins	7
The Voyage of Emma Darwin	11
Victor the Wild Boy	36
In the Air Pump	38
Reinventing the Globe	39
Coelacanths	40
The Rise and Fall of Albert Einstein	41
Neanderthals	42
National Curriculum 2020	43
Clinging to the Diction	44
Playing for an Oscar	45
The Descent of Michelangelo	49
A Cleaning Job	50
A Final Cleansing	51
Reconstructing Leonardo	52

AUTHOR'S NOTE

The first poem sequence in this collection, 'Origins', engages with Charles Darwin's *The Origin of Species* (1859): its inception, its impact, and the resulting spiritual estrangement. The second, 'The Voyage of Emma Darwin', charts similar territory from a more domestic and feminine perspective. Much of the material in the extracts from Emma's fictitious private journal, as well as that in the family letters, has been drawn from *Emma Darwin: A Century of Family Letters*, edited by Henrietta Litchfield (John Murray, 1915), and *Darwin* by Adrian Desmond and James Moore (Michael Joseph, 1991).

When Charles Darwin married his first cousin Emma Wedgwood at St Peter's Church, Maer, on 29 January 1839, he was 30 and she 31. The Darwin family seat was about 30 miles away in Shrewsbury. The couple first settled in London before moving to Down House in Kent. Charles was from a more freethinking tradition than Emma, who was steeped in Anglican respectability and thought that religious faith was not to be questioned. Yet by contemporary standards both their families were liberal and tolerant. Charles died in 1882 and Emma in 1896 at the age of 88.

The concluding sequence, 'Reconstructing Leonardo', takes the form of a succession of epiphanic 'scenes' in the career of that enigmatic and versatile Renaissance artist, Leonardo da Vinci. Some of the poems are spoken by people who knew him or worked with him, as though being interviewed for a TV documentary. Like his own painting, *The Last Supper*, the sequence exhibits a formal dramatic symmetry. The central monologue and the only one spoken by Leonardo himself, 'The Dream', reflects the centrality of Christ in the painting flanked on either side by the various gestures of the twelve disciples, while the final poem shifts the perspective abruptly to one of the typically meticulous obsessions of the present age.

ORIGINS

1 *The Individual*

*'I have attempted to write the following account of
myself as if I were a dead man in another world looking
back at my own life.'*
                    Charles Darwin (1809–82), Autobiography

Four years old: Caroline peeling an orange,
humming softly and rocking, playfully
sliding each segment over my lips
as I sat on her knee.

A shape at the window – a bull
from the meadow – startled and caused me
to tumble, catching my wrist on the knife.

This was before the quest into life.

Of my mother I remember hardly a thing.
I was always much slower in learning
than Catherine or Caroline.
My sisters were warm, loving, but kept so much in.

This was before the loneliness turning.

I loved to spin fables from things I had seen
in the wood: once told a boy how orchids
grew any colour I happened to choose
by feeding them liquids of various hues.

This was before I understood.

At school I became an avid collector
of curious facts, birds' eggs, minerals, beetles –
found three, quite rare, while climbing a tree.
In zeal I popped them into my mouth,
scrambling down.

This was before they spoke to me.

My brother Erasmus mastered science and art,
his confidence firm, his intellect sharp.
I was always so hazy and ponderous,
never quite sure where to tread.

I studied for medicine but could not dissect
or stand by the surgeon and not be distressed.

This was before the blessing of chloroform.

I prepared for the clergy, spurred on by phrenology,
due to the shape of my head.

This was before the dawning of reason.

A letter concerning the *Beagle* arrested my fall.
My father, the wisest man I have known,
allowed me to choose.

This was before the wonder of seeing.

This was before the storm.

2 *The Species*

'There are not as many men living on the surface of the globe as animalcules in the sperm of a single male.'
                    Anton van Leeuwenhoek (1632–1723)

We saw the preformed being in our seed.
Each one housed another, a perfect line,
undefiled: a living creed.

We found ourselves supreme above the beasts,
supported by an incarnation science
could not reach: saw ourselves as priests

of some unswerving law conceived
upon a single breath, could not shift
the logic of a Russian doll that cleaved

upon an image rushing outwards
from our Father's hand.
We were suddenly divided by our words,

stricken by a text fragmented, incomplete:
a branching metamorphosis that leavened us
with chance our paraclete.

We glimpsed the sightless author of contingency:
a world we had subdued became
a proving ground exploding with uncertainty.

What vast ancestral comforter will stumble
from this grief as our descendants sleep?
What Russian doll will tumble?

3 *The Transmission*

*'I have called this principle, by which each slight variation,
if useful, is preserved, by the term of Natural Selection.'*
          Charles Darwin, *The Origin of Species*

Incunabula and scribe,
I have no face:
your image is unique
in time and space.

I act without a conscience
or a goal:
accumulative change
is my control.

The anodyne of dreams
now bids me speak
and turn your troubled mind
to my critique.

Reason gave you cause
to seek my hand
and through it you begin
to understand.

With each passing moment
of your quest
I lag behind, enfeebled,
dispossessed.

You are the first to be allowed
beyond my reach:
the swiftness of your journey
rests on speech.

A passage into myth
gave some respite:
space to see direction
in your flight.

Science took you further
on your course,
unravelling the distance
from your source.

Never has a race
gained such a view
of that which gave them muscle,
bone and sinew.

Incunabula and scribe,
I have no face.
You are the first to be released
from my embrace.

THE VOYAGE OF EMMA DARWIN

Charles to Emma

                                                                      Shrewsbury
                                                                      Nov. 15 1838

My Dear Emma,

Where to begin;
my good fortune
is undeserved.
Like a spoilt child
I can only echo
Father's words,
'You have drawn a prize!'
May I prove worthy
of such a prize.

After life at Maer
evenings may be dull:
all men are brutes
and you are marrying
a solitary brute.
Show my letters
to no one – uncertainty
and disbelief
creep through me

like a worm.

Emma to her Aunt Jessie in Paris

                                            Maer
                                            Nov. 16 1838

My Dear Aunt Jessie,

When you enquired of Charles
I was unsure of his feelings
and on my return from Paris
he seemed so far away.
I now know he was unwell.

He asked me on Thursday.
Imagine! I told only Papa,
Mamma and Elizabeth –
if only you saw
the tears of joy!

Mamma is all trousseaux,
wedding cake, invitations –
endless trouble and expense.
Charles abides pomp
even less than I.

He is so open, every word
reflecting true thoughts.
Nor is he fastidious,
but affectionate, sweet-tempered,
humane to animals.

He avoids wine, dislikes drama,
but stands concerts very well.
I was to have been asked
in August, but he was afraid –
a most unnecessary fear.

Emma to Charles

> Maer
> Jan. 7 1839

My Dear Charley,

I beg you, be careful,
fearful even, of casting off
what Jesus has done.
It would be a nightmare
were we not united forever.

Never conceal anything
to spare me pain:
we now belong to each other
and I too must speak out.
Will you do me a favour?

Read the 13th Chapter
of St John – so full
of tender devotion. Indulge me
in this whim – it would mean
more than words can say.

I write for my own good
as much as your own –
no need to answer this.
I am presumptuous, but reason alone
does not lead to revelation.

Charles to Emma

                                          Macaw Cottage, Gower St
                                          London
                                          Jan. 20 1839

My Dear Emma,

The house is almost ready;
everything in place except
a few drawers of shells.
The garden, you will agree,
is worth its weight in gold.

I often wonder why solitude
suits me: on my voyage
all pleasure came from thought –
in desert, forest, or at night
pacing the deck of the *Beagle*.

You may humanise me yet –
even this ferocious passion
for accumulating facts,
analysing, theorising,
leaving me completely

without boundaries.

Journal Extract

Dec. 21 1839

We have grown closer
yet it keeps returning,
sweeping over me
from some awful
unimaginable distance:

          even now
in this quiet house
where love buoys my heart,
hope quells my fear,
new life quickens –

I am being tethered
to the far side
of faith, where I wait,
an exile
in a crumbling land.

This bright room –
its prints, books,
chairs, pianoforte
dissolving
on a sea of chaos.

Fortitude, duty, compassion
will guide me: nothing
shall die while I live.
May those in peril
turn to me.

Emma to her Aunt Jessie in Paris

> Macaw Cottage, Gower St
> London
> Feb. 10 1840

My Dear Aunt Jessie,

A safe delivery, thank Heaven!
Willy has blue eyes, a pretty mouth,
a nose I cannot boast of, though
harmless enough while so tiny.

Charles spends hours peering
into the cot, making notes
on every expression. Even a looking-glass
has been pressed into service.

Like the rest of the world
I am reading Carlyle – his pamphlet
on Chartism is quite unreasonable
and puts out one's patience.

His conversation, however,
is most engaging – unlike his wife's
hysterical giggle. Charles thinks her
un-ladylike, a view I also share.

We are delighted you are coming
to England. I well remember my bright,
happy stay in Paris. Must go now
to feed Willy, play for Charles.

Journal Extract

Aug. 16 1842

Out in the streets
Chartists are rioting
for higher wages, the vote,
a secret ballot: it is not safe
to venture forth.

We are moving
to an uncharted place:
fixed bayonets
cannot hold them.
'Remember, we are brothers.'

Yes.
Brothers without reason
or reverence; stability
requires both.
We are hemmed in

by a great gulf
of envy, malice, threat.
What world will Willy
and Annie inherit?
What secret will hold them?

Emma to her Aunt Jessie at Tenby

>   Down House
>   Kent
>   Aug. 27 1845

My Dear Aunt Jessie,

We are undertaking great earthworks
for a new kitchen garden. The house
is snugger for the coming winter,
the servants' quarters more comfortable:
seems selfish to withhold the benefits
of increasing prosperity. Charles
has revised his Journal: it is improved
greatly, with many things left out and others,
of more interest, now included. He has
again taken up the essay on species.
Thankfully, on the question of publication,
our reluctance is equal. Though our reasons,
my dear Aunt, differ somewhat.

Charles to Emma

                                              Shrewsbury
                                              May 27 1848

My Dear Wife,

So glad of your account
of the new baby; am reassured
to know Elizabeth is there.
I am still weak, but improving.
The attack was quite sudden.

The children sound splendid:
seems Annie is a second Mozart.
Her Wedgwood blood will win,
I am sure, many hearts.
What a pity she cannot sing.

Father had a peaceful night,
became cheerful at cards.
Anxiety, though, fills each day.
He always says how comfortable
he now is; a great blessing.

I am in the summerhouse watching
the approach of a thunderstorm.
A break in the stifling heat
is long overdue. I yearn
to be safely back in your arms.

Do kiss Willy, Annie, George
and Etty for me. The blackcaps
here sing beautifully: right now
I could not give two hoots
how they were formed.

Journal Extract

                                          Jan. 19 1849

I know why he trembles,
why despondency, dizziness, sickness
claw at his flesh;
why the fainting, the sweating,
the sharp palpitations and black spots
in front of his eyes
come and go.

I know these afflictions
and wrap them in scripture and prayer.
I can only bear witness
to ease the transition within.
I know why he trembles,
I know why his eyes
grow so dim.

Charles to Emma

> Malvern Hydropathic Home
> April 23 1851

My Dearest Emma,

I pray God you are prepared.
Our own dear Annie went
most sweetly, to her final sleep
at twelve o'clock today.
God knows what miseries
might have been in store for her.
I cannot recall a single moment
of admonishment. Towards the end
she made pathetic attempts
to sing. Do what you can
to bear up: let us be thankful
for the daguerreotype.

Emma to Charles

> Down House
> Kent
> April 24 1851

Dearest Charley,

When no message came yesterday
I knew full well the meaning.
This loss obliterates
all that went before,
leaves me painfully indifferent
to the other children.
Yours is the only comfort
I crave – she concealed not
a thought from us, was so open
and affectionate. Poor Willy;
he takes it all so quietly
as if it happened long ago.

Journal Extracts

June 3 1851

As one burden descends
another begins to lift:
I move more easily
on this shifting tide.

It all happened long ago
and it is catching up,
unfastening us, unravelling
this unimaginable distance.

*

June 17 1851

Etty has just asked me,
'Mamma, where do the women
go to, for the angels
are all men?'

We go where our hearts
may survive, piecing together
our crumbling lands
from afar, with empty words.

Journal Extracts

                              Aug. 2 1851

The Great Exhibition
has left me quite breathless:
whirling pumps, presses,
clattering looms, hissing engines.

Crystal Palace, it seems,
is our new shrine of science.
But erected by angels
or by brutes?

                    *

                              Dec. 16 1854

In the Crimea, I understand,
Flo Nightingale astonishes
the finest surgeons
with her presence of mind.

Soldiers, I believe,
kiss her shadow as it moves
over their beds:
this news brings with it

wider consolation.

Charles to Emma

> Moor Park Hydropathic Home
> Surrey
> April 15 1857

My Dear Wife,

Good thing you packed me off here;
really is most unaccountable
how sprightly I feel – walking
and eating like a hearty Christian.

That everlasting species book
seems, at times, beyond my powers.
Have hardly thought of it until
loitering in the park today:

while amusing myself with ants
I stumbled on a great find –
the rare slave-making species.
Have sent them off for confirmation.

I received, yesterday, some fine skins
from that capital fellow Alfred Wallace,
though the carriage cost a fortune.
We appear to have much common ground.

Still have six longish letters to write,
so will close now, dearest of wives.

Journal Extract

                              Nov. 22 1859

Today the storm breaks: lightning
and church bells will peal.
1500 copies will be too few.

He cannot be wrong, no man
spends more time on the question
of change – yet how forsaken
I now feel, having ministered
to the guttering light lost
in animal obsession, having stifled
my soul to meet the swell
of reason, having nurtured life
to have it snatched by darkness,
having kindled hope to have it
crushed by treason.

Today the storm breaks: lightning
and church bells will peal.
1500 copies will be too few.

Emma to the Editor of 'The Spectator'

> Down House
> Kent
> Oct. 24 1862

Sir,

Those who sympathise with suffering animals
must feel satisfaction at the warm interest
lately excited on the subject of vivisection.
However, there is a suffering inflicted not
in the cause of science, but in amusement:
on the great estates of this country steel traps
are daily laid to catch vermin, which invade
our game-preserves to prey on stock.
If we could but know the pain felt
by such a hapless beast – to have a limb
crushed for a whole night between iron teeth,
the agony increased by attempts to escape –
we would perhaps pause. Yet thousands thus linger
every night. Must we also linger in indifference?
I cannot accept that English gentlemen,
who are neither blind nor vindictive,
are unable to devise a more humane method
than this grisly instrument now in use.

Journal Extracts

                                Jan. 14 1864

For twenty-seven days in a row
he has vomited after every meal –
too weak to raise a pen, I take
dictation, recording the habits
of poison ivy, purple loosestrife,
bryony, clematis, Indian cress.

The greenhouse, hallway, study
seethe with slow vegetable life.
I move beneath a canopy of runners,
tendrils, leaves. All rates of growth
are measured, all deviations logged,
all fertile crosses

described, marked, isolated.

                    *

                                May 5 1864

Captain Fitzroy of the *Beagle*
has been found dead, his throat
slit open: beside his body
a complimentary copy of the *Origin*.

Emma to her Aunt Fanny at Tenby

London
April 28 1866

Dearest Aunt Fanny,

Last night I accompanied Charles
to the Royal Society: his beard
so alters his appearance he passed
quite unnoticed. The Prince of Wales –
a good-natured youth, most polite –
is so softly spoken, Charles
missed every word said to him
so bowed profoundly and moved on.

Have just finished reading
*The Lancashire Wedding or Darwin
Moralised* – the moral being
it is foolish to give up a healthy,
poor girl you love for a sickly,
rich one you despise. The plot
is dull, tedious, far too obvious
and ought to have been reversed.

Charles relaxes as best he can:
if only he could smoke a pipe
or ruminate like a cow.
Our Persian kitten is charming –
always smudging her face into mine.
Even now I miss Aunt Jessie:
the world is so changed I fear
she would hardly recognise it.

Journal Extract

July 12 1868

Have lately been unsure what rules I ought to follow
in keeping Sunday holy.

On the side of abstaining from what others think wrong:

Fear of loosening religious sanctions: many
do not distinguish the breaking of observances
from actual sin.

On the side of doing as you are led, regardless of opinion:

The sincerity of appearing as you really are.

The good it would do the world to have no artificial sins.

That England would be morally bettered for Sunday amusements.

That the servants may learn the value of toleration.

These things apply only to myself: am most reluctant
to interfere with the pleasures of sons the age mine are.

Charles to his Daughter Henrietta at Cannes

> Down House
> Kent
> April 28 1871

My Dear Old Etty,

Murray has reprinted 2000 copies
of *The Descent of Man*, ensuring
4500 for this edition.
Have received almost no abuse
(except a Welshman calling me
a thick-skulled, hairy old ape).

Reviewers already talk of the lucid,
vigorous style: in this respect
I cannot thank you enough
for the arrangement, the aids
in the reasoning and unending
corrections of grammar.

Wallace's review shows clearly
what small influence I now have
with him, though in future
the Wallace–Darwin episode
will surely form a bright spot
amongst rival claimants.

What an awful, astounding fact
that you are soon to be married.
There is no hope for that but to
hold Mother as an example:
in time to come your husband
will both love and worship you.

You will not feel properly married
until you are in your own home.
It is the furniture that does the job.

Journal Extract

> Jan. 17 1874

We have been to a séance
with Wallace, Huxley, Francis Galton
and George Eliot.

As curtains were drawn
we joined hands, while the medium
swayed to and fro
slowly, for what seemed an entire age.

Charley soon tired, lost all patience
and dragged himself away.

There was a sound
of rushing wind; a candlestick
jumped from the table, sparks flashed
across the ceiling, the table itself
began to rise, as if carried
by an invisible current.

We stood back, astonished, silent.

When he returned, the chairs
were piled onto the table.

'Lord have mercy on us
if we have to swallow such rubbish!'

Yet the moving of furniture is nothing
beside the creak of a closing mind.

Emma to her Son William in Southampton

Cambridge
Nov. 18 1877

My Dear Willy,

The Senate House was packed yesterday
for Father's Honorary Degree. Undergraduates
spilled from the galleries, perched
on statues and stood in the windows.
He was ushered in to the accompaniment
of a deafening roar; for a moment
I thought he would be overcome, but no.
He beamed back at them. Then a cord
was strung across the chamber and a monkey
was released, causing even greater uproar.
A Proctor climbed up to catch it, though
I think it escaped and vanished somewhere.
The Vice-Chancellor then appeared
amidst much bowing and hand-shaking
before Father marched down the aisle
led by two men holding silver maces.
When the speech ended a few words in Latin
were spoken, then everyone rushed forward
with most hearty congratulations.

Of all days in the year to have a headache –
though I enjoyed it all; felt very grand
with my LL.D. in his red silk gown.

Journal Extracts

                                              Nov. 7 1879

My sister Elizabeth died today:
her year-long illness had been
so distressing I feel only joy –
blind, delirious, bedridden,
her life ended long ago.
I will hear forever the frail
bewilderment of her final words:

'Where is Emma?'

                           *

                                             June 11 1880

He is now training earthworms,
though without great progress
as they neither see nor hear
but spend hours seizing hold
of the edge of a cabbage leaf,
trying to pull it into their holes.
They give such feeble tugs yet manage

to shake the whole leaf.

Emma to her Son William in Southampton

>Down House
>Kent
>Nov. 23 1881

My Dear Willy,

Father is at last rewarded
for months at the microscope –
something new is emerging
about the structure of roots.

The supervision of dormitories
in French schools is admirable:
boys ought not to indulge
in uproarious games after dark.

When they are fully grown
they will do as they please,
but early restraint will ensure
stability in manhood.

This view horrifies Father,
but if bullying takes place
it will be in the hours
when no one is watching.

I live in the past, Willy,
and want no more discovery.
Father, as you well know,
never tires of it.

Our grandchildren, I trust,
will have more certain guidance
as this strange new age
begins to shed its light.

Journal Extract

April 19 1882

The end came at four o'clock this afternoon.
Blood trickled into his beard as brutal pain
tossed his heaving body into spasm. His skin
turned cold and grey, his deep, rich voice
became thin, hollow, almost childlike:

'I am not the least afraid, Emma.'

I held him to my breast, swaying gently.
Bird-song filled the air. Afterwards I walked
into the garden. I remember the sun dazzling
my eyes, warming my skin. On reaching
his favourite footpath I stooped

to gather a bouquet of wild lilies.

VICTOR THE WILD BOY

Loosely based upon a true story

Spoke not a word
in my short life.
I'll tell from the grave
my obituary.

Lived in the woods
on berries and roots.
Knew nothing till now
of my ancestry.

Slept with the wolves,
curled against cold.
Acquired their harsh
ingenuity.

Was captured at twelve
by a man with a smile.
Told me that speech
would set me free.

Took me away
to a place without trees.
Said I would find
my destiny.

Taught me to sleep
away from the sky.
Said I was part
of society.

Showed me some cards
full of strange marks.
Told me that words
were my only key.

Couldn't quite utter
the sounds he made.
Couldn't unlock
the sanctuary.

Sent me away
to a place without grass.
Said I would never
find harmony.

Was left in a cell
to dream of the wolves.
'An idiot lost
in his savagery.'

Saw a great light
piercing the dark.
Carried my soul
to victory.

Saw my parents
covered in shame.
Said that they tried
to murder me.

Down to the woods,
slit my throat.
Left me there
at the age of three.

Spoke not a word
in my short life.
I was the fruit
of treachery.

Two Poems on Paintings by Joseph Wright of Derby (1734–97)

IN THE AIR PUMP

An Experiment on a Bird in the Air Pump

A white cockatoo gasps for breath
in the thin transparent globe of reason
as the pivotal arm of the philosopher
weighs the uncertain moment
from the subdued glow of a newly framed question.

To his left a father comforts
two small daughters, distressed, not yet aware
of the boldness of the times.

To the left again a man ponders
inevitabilities, losses, the play of light
on a human skull resting
in a bowl of water.

                    To his right
a love-struck couple, oblivious of the drama
of air, glass, feathers, see only themselves
emerging from the enclosed spaces
of the familiar.

At the window's dark margin a boy,
glimpsed only by the moon, awaits a signal
to lower the cage; opposite him
another, hungry mind agog with the cool
harsh vacuum poised above.

In the foreground a man engaged solely
in counting each second of suffocation.

REINVENTING THE GLOBE

A Philosopher Giving a Lecture on the Orrery

Here are the orbits, their precise
irresistible laws – everything
calculated, ordained, inviolate:
well-dressed men of science,
planets of polished brass.
The rococo flourish of silk, velvet, satin
eclipsed by the sleek fluttering whirr
of Newtonian clockwork.

Here is the burgeoning globe
of reason, reinventing itself,
breaking the limits of its own trajectory.
An infinitesimal earth rotates
on the gleaming planetarium
like a pinball. Tilt the canvas –
the whole thing lights up,
the question about to be answered.

COELACANTHS

Seventy fathoms down
balletic blue fish six feet long
rehearse a four hundred million year ritual.

Lobe-finned, complacent, crepuscular,
moving with great paddle-like motions
over lava-flows, sometimes backwards,
sometimes belly-up, sometimes drifting
nose-down with the current, honing
the repertoire of a bizarre masque.

Seventy fathoms down
before the amphibians, the reptiles,
the mammals, the apes; us.

Giving birth to fully formed young
with the stubborn muscular resistance
of myth, they dance across the strata
unaccompanied, bulbous fleshy tails
waving as they approach: metronomes
ticking to a silent repetitious score.

Seventy fathoms down
a spotlight from a redesigned submersible
catches the last performance

for the archives.

THE RISE AND FALL OF ALBERT EINSTEIN

1879–1955

He succumbed at last to the newshounds,
the formal dinners and speeches,
yet remained, like his science,
a treacherous enigma:
a German who despised Germans,
a pacifist who pushed deterrence,
a Jew who showed that time itself
was suspect.

Once it had all been very low-key:
assessing patents in a tiny office
at Berne, equations and loose change
over frugal café lunches.
But that was long ago
before the physicist emerged equipped
at all points – aloof, eccentric,
unbudgeable.

Before the embittered flight
from Berlin, wandering Gandhi-like
along the clear corridor of conscience
to Oxford: everywhere he looked
there was colossal gravity.
He almost became an Englishman but,
like all inessentials, the thought drifted,
the light sped past.

Physics melted in his mouth
and the world crumbled at his feet.
In the end the indeterminacy of the atom
caught him out: not even Princeton
could shore him up.
He had come to an absolute rest
in his own space
and in his own time.

NEANDERTHALS

A numbing succession of flint axes,
a fifty thousand year humdrum heartbeat.

What fictive inner voice abstaining
on the curve of humanity gave them a world?

With no rethink, counterthink, doublethink
they were rooted in like trees.

Art, ritual, symbol, myth
would have been mere tautology.

So different from those tall restless invaders
with too many voices, too many worlds.

Yet the striking edge of a fresh flake of obsidian
can be as thin as a single molecule.

NATIONAL CURRICULUM 2020

A small boy listens
to something he cannot grasp,
something unsettling:
at the heart of everything
particles dance unpredictably,
sidestepping the choreographies
of Newton, Einstein, threatening
to skip past even Hawking.

He stares at the screen's
simulated quantum blur,
the nervous twitching
of leptons, muons, quarks.
Outside, sycamore seeds
pirouette past the window
with the calm unfaltering certainty
of St Francis.

CLINGING TO THE DICTION

'In 1775 we behold him to great advantage; his degree of Master of Arts conferred upon him, his dictionary published, his correspondence animated, his benevolence exercised.'
James Boswell, The Life of Samuel Johnson

Glimpse too the undertow of dread
in that vast sea of words:
the speech of the ghost in *Hamlet*
terrified him as a boy; now everywhere
his closest friends were sinking fast.

Watch him bareheaded in drizzling rain
at the site of his father's bookstall
tasting the shame
as he refused to serve – beneath him
when every penny mattered.

Years of grime and hackwork
showed how much: when thrift alone
could not dig his mother's grave
wrote *Rasselas* in one cramped week;
a conclusion in which nothing was resolved.

Peer into the Fleet Street attic –
limp annotated volumes stacked
across the floor; a counting-house
of definitions sagging
under the entry to his wife's death.

A king's pension lifted only
the pen's burden: failing health
fattened the black dog of melancholy.
In that spacious rational mind
dust and monsters settled like a ransom.

Look up Samuel Johnson –
what does it say? Poet, essayist,
scholar, philanthropist, lexicographer:
a harmless drudge whose etymology
is forgotten.

PLAYING FOR AN OSCAR

'In so vulgar an age as this we all need masks.'
Oscar Wilde (1854–1900)

Act 1

The curtain was rising, as were the eyebrows,
even at Oxford: laying a man out cold
for sneering at his verse, squandering his allowance
on blue and white china – convention
he was born to defy, while success,
like everything but alcohol,
went straight to his head.

Before a single ticket was sold
fame released him from the tyranny of boredom
into the lap of preposterous opulence:
taking cabs to cross the street,
a lover's arm to cross the lounge.
London arrived fawning over Oscar –
immense, unconcerned, immaculately lazy.

In America he took a standing ovation
and came back flat broke: the wit
never faltered – immortal one-liners
tumbling from his lips like housemaids' gossip.
Rumours began early; in spite of marriage,
in spite of children: behind lacquered scenery
lurked secrets, raptures, wrongdoing.

As each scene unfolded backstage scandal
reverberated through the wings; first nights
threatened to become unstoppable:
laughter, applause, prosperity
took indiscretion into unprecedented places.
He had after all the leading role –
indulgent, gay, liberal, believing everything

should have a trial.

Act 2

He always wore a soft suede glove
    To cushion the rapier wit
And malice they could never find
    As they dragged him through the pit:
The closing scene was under way
    And still he would not quit.

He spoke with a lilting nasal air
    To the lawyers and the judge:
The jury stalled, the trial stopped,
    And still he would not budge.
So they turned the hilt of the legal knife
    With a two-year penal trudge.

He heard a voice in the prison yard
    Whispering words of dew:
'I'm sorry, Guv, I truly am.
    It's 'ard for the likes of you.'
'No my friend, we suffer alike
    And each man pays his due.'

The sentence passed, he fled to France –
    An exile with no name:
The dazzling role he made his own
    Had scorched him with its flame,
While all about him faces turned
    In fear of mortal shame.

He'd never known the world to look
    With such a spiteful eye
Upon the part he now rehearsed
    Beneath a blackened sky;
For they had killed the life he craved
    And so he had to die.

*

In Père Lachaise there is a place
   Where countless souls have filed
Past Balzac, Bizet, Chopin –
   Half-absent as they smiled,
While countless more have sadly knelt
   At the grave of Oscar Wilde.

Act 3

No one could be certain of the colour of his eyes
for it seemed to change with the light.

He moved languidly, reluctantly, bloodless and corpulent,
his coarse skin always clean-shaven.

The luxurious handshake, lacking grip,
would often repel under the ironic smile.

The face was magisterial, masklike,
by turns sinister, radiant, disdainful, amorous.

Sometimes a scarab-ringed forefinger was crooked
across the mouth, concealing crowded uneven teeth.

There was always a buttonhole, usually violets,
often carnations – occasionally green.

His gestures, inevitable yet memorably effective,
were remarkably slight.

In mixed company he produced enormous ambivalence:
alone with either sex he was irresistible.

Impeccable precision characterised his diction
yet facts were of no importance to him.

The rhythmic audacity of his speech swung instantly
from trenchant wit to the most elaborate reverie.

No one could be certain of the colour of his eyes.
But he had the voice, even from the beginning,

of a fallen angel.

THE DESCENT OF MICHELANGELO

Look at my face – ugly,
exhausted, creased with toil.
I've traipsed through Italy
a thousand times for the love of God.
Now I'm old, my heart empty.
A hornet circles in my head,
beetles rattle in my gut.
In one ear a spider's web,
in the other a cricket sings all night.

With my mother's milk I swallowed
hammers, chisels, chunks of marble.
Look closer – those yellow flecks
in my eyes – flaws in the strata.
From a botched discarded stone
I delivered the statue of David:
it moved to the Palazzo
erect, pensive – suspended
above fifty shouting men.

In the dust and blistering heat
of innumerable candles I painted
the Sistine vault –
head craned backwards
like a hungry bird
fresh from the egg.
The whole world flocked
as fury, concentrated,
pumped through my veins.

Feel my skin – limp
and coarse as sackcloth:
when I take off my boots
it sloughs like a snake's.
Rome – a compost heap
writhing with good and evil.
Tap my skull. Silence.
I've traversed the sea of Heaven
to drown in a cesspool.

A CLEANING JOB

They are separating the darkness
from the ceiling.

A curtained scaffold hangs under the cracked
and grimy arm of God:

distilled water is sponged on,
antibacterial gel brushed in.

It will take them nine years.
Michelangelo took only four.

Vinyl resin is pumped into weak plaster,
filling a threatening void:

the restorer's credo, like the physician's:
First, do no harm.

But can a pulse be detectable
after nearly five hundred years?

A final layer of gel is rinsed off:
embedded in the surface like stubble –

bristles from his own brush
and small indentations along the wrist of Adam

where he tested the set of the plaster
with his fingertips.

A FINAL CLEANSING

Michelangelo's athletic angels,
tormented sinners, leering demons
can finally breathe –

redemption and damnation are at last
held in check
by the precise judgement
of discreet electronic sensors:

humidity, temperature, dust content –

every gasp of awe stripped clean

by the pulsing of a tiny current.

RECONSTRUCTING LEONARDO

'And things will descend with fury from above,
and will give us nourishment and light.'
                    Leonardo da Vinci (1452–1519)

1 *Ser Piero's Tale*

What more could I do?
Marry Caterina, an untutored peasant?
Such things are not done.

That the boy inherited her charm and beauty
is self-evident:
his fortitude, thankfully, is all mine.

But there is something more:
a relentless curiosity
in every living thing he encounters.

As if a perfect copy
were not enough.
What he hopes to achieve is beyond me.

Which is why I brought him
to Andrea del Verrochio –
finest craftsman in Florence.

What alternative did I have?
University, medicine, law
were out of the question.

As for Caterina, he will soon forget.

2 *The Gift*

In a darkened workshop
a single beam of light
strikes a wooden shield,
freshly painted.

On a bench
lie bats, lizards,
crickets, snakes – dissected,
recombined.

Dust particles dance
in the sun's thin shaft
as shutters tremble
to a sharp rap.

The door
is eased open:
Ser Piero steps in,
sees a monstrous beast –

venom oozing
from its mouth, fire
in its eyes, smoke
trailing from its nostrils.

'What is this, Leonardo?'

'This is what a shield
is supposed to do.

Take it, Father.'

3 Verrochio's Tale

You see this panel?
This was the last time I used a brush.
The angel to the right is my own
but to the left – this is Leonardo.
We used the Flemish method –
paints crushed and mixed
not with egg-yolk, but oil
giving imperceptible gradations of colour.

Look at the garments –
another new technique.
Rags dipped in plaster, draped
over clay figures then drawn
on white linen with the point of a brush.
And the landscape, you see?
Shining amber lake, receding
stretch of hills – Leonardo's world.

He worked slowly – obstinate
to the last. Any other apprentice
would have incurred my wrath.
But to be angry with him
was impossible –
he commanded affection.
His lucid reasoning disarmed
and confounded all who listened.

He came to me
with everything to learn:
in a few years had outstripped
even his master. After this painting
I confined myself to sculpture.

4 *The Descent*

'Tomorrow morning I shall make
the attempt…'

The wings – pinewood
strengthened with lime,
the pulleys leather
treated with alum.
Reeds control the rudder,
young pine laths
form the chassis.

'I will experiment with this machine
over a lake…'

Sized silk covers the frame.
The wingspan is ten metres,
the weight one hundred kilos.
Over his shoulders –
a leather harness,
around his waist
a large wineskin filled with air.

'A bird functions according
to mathematical laws…'

For a brief moment
the wind carries him.
The landscape tilts
then veers away
leaving clear sky.
He listens
to flapping silk, crumpling wood.

The landscape roars past,
drowning his thoughts.

5 *A Friar's Tale*

I saw him often
in those days: as the sun
began its ascent
he would arrive
at the monastery, go straight
to the refectory and mount
his ingenious scaffolding.

Many days would see him
from dawn to dusk
forgetting to eat or drink,
continually working.
But with Leonardo,
of course,
one could never tell.

Sometimes, when the sun
was at its height
he would rush in
like a madman,
put in one or two strokes,
then leave, brimming
with sullen disdain.

But he could also linger
for days on end
without touching a brush.
Standing before *The Last Supper*
he would examine
each disciple, questioning
every gesture and expression.

Once, as he passed by
I caught a glimpse
of the faltering uncertainty
in those piercing blue-green eyes.

6 *The Visit*

An old man is dying
in the hospital of Santa Maria Novello.
He has lived a hundred years,
he says; feels no more sorrow,
only weakness.

Leonardo draws closer,
his hair brushing the withered cheek.
'Tell me,' he whispers,
'can these things really
have an end?'

The old man smiles
as if the question were an answer,
closes his eyes on the world
and the insistent stranger
leaning over him.

Outside, children laugh,
play, shout. Dogs, pigs, goats
mingle with the crowds
as early evening
lengthens every shadow.

*

Desperate for sleep,
Leonardo cuts through the empty blackness
of Milan: under his arm
meticulous diagrams
of vessels, arteries, the heart.

7 The Dream

I am a young boy wandering
the vineyards of Vinci; the air
pungent with orange groves as I stumble
over twisted roots to a hillside scree
of fractured rock veined with silver.

Through a screen of tangled vine
a cave compels me to explore.
I stoop, spellbound, peering hard
into the dark – left hand
easing apart the sinewy wood.

My muscles stiffen – fear and desire
allowing neither entry nor retreat.
Marvellous things await discovery;
strange relics, ancient forms.
My head pounds in the blistering heat.

In the air above a terrible geometry
of sound and light sends me crashing
to the ground – a kite flushed with red
and muted gold settles on my chest,
forcing its tail into my parched mouth.

I am younger still, playing
at the feet of Albiera, my stepmother –
the cool rustle of her dress like water
flowing past. She lifts me to the window.
A kite hovers for a moment, then is gone.

And I am being suckled at the breast
of Caterina, steeped in a world
of syllable and touch. Her fingers
ripple through the soft down
along the backs of my arms.

8 Machiavelli's Tale

I was struck by his obsession.
He was military engineer
to Cesare Borgia
and seemed out of place
until conversation brought us closer.
For in the mind of this ageing artist
was a passion and rigour
I had long aspired to.

During bitter winter evenings
he laid bare the mechanics
of weaponry and ballistics,
showed me detailed plans
of mortars, a colossal crossbow,
even winged projectiles:
machines to bring dread
to the most resilient enemy.

Yet for all his ambition
the malevolence of war haunted him.
Nor could he deal in guile
when fortune favoured it.
For he was obsessed not with power
or principality, but with peace:
an arbiter whose one allegiance
was life.

I envied him.

9 *The Sitter*

She is thinking of her child:
his death in infancy a year ago
had taken its toll; she had wanted
to join him, slicing her wrists.

Francesco, her husband, withdrew
from business, turned away from art:
the bright colours of their lives
rinsed away by grief.

This painter, though, brings out
soft outlines, subdued tones,
catching the eggshell delicacy
of the bloom beneath the shadow.

In the filtered sunlight
of a screened-off courtyard
Leonardo moves through her mind
like a blur.

She is learning to smile.

10 Michelangelo's Tale

If you want something finished
don't turn to Leonardo:
he never carries a work through
without a thousand interventions
and afterthoughts.
But come inside, the wind is keen.

Here in Rome you must fight
for recognition – it's teeming
with artists jostling for a place:
reputations made and broken
on the whim of a pope.
And where is Leonardo in all this?

I'll tell you: hiding in that villa
designing curving mirrors.
Why? To view the stars
with the aid of some great reflector!
If I squandered my talent like that
I wouldn't presume to criticise.

Yesterday he saw the nude figures
on my recent fresco.
You know what he compared them to?
Bags of nuts and bunches of radishes!
Smug, erratic, unreliable. But enough of him.
Look up, tell me what you think.

11 *The Self-Portrait*

He sits within three mirrors:
one facing him, one three-quarters on,
one behind: between his fingers
soft chalk the colour of rust.
All his teeth are gone.
Obliquely he begins to see
the gaunt reflection of sixty years:
Caterina, Ser Piero, Albiera, Verrochio.

The expression follows in his wake:
flared nostrils and full lips
give way to disillusioned lines
around the mouth. Sharp eyes
gaze downward under thick brows,
interrogative, indecisive, resigned.
The flowing patriarchal beard
trails off into bitterness.

The face stares past him
from the tinted paper: he holds it
closer to the guttering candles.
This stranger came forth
from the shades of night.
What would it matter if he burns?
Who would salvage what the world
turns away from?

One by one the candles go out.

12 *The Tale of the King of France*

Francis the First (1515–47)

In those last few years at Amboise
he came to accept himself:
as his left arm became useless,
instead of complaining, began
to sort through his notes – the eye
and vision, the movement of water,
anatomy, painting, engineering,
rock formation, the flight of birds.

All his life he sought answers
that are beyond us. As for myself
I simply enjoyed his conversation:
he had seen and done so many
extraordinary things – once showed me
the bones of a huge sea monster
dug from a canal, reconstructed it
in front of my eyes.

After his burial I discovered
plans for a circular staircase,
had my architects adapt it
for the new château at Chambord.
Nothing like it has ever been seen.
How he came upon this design
mystifies me, like everything about him:
a double helix.

13 *The Restorer*

She wields scalpel, paintbrush, microscope
with a surgeon's skill, removing dirt, mould,
layers of paint from past resuscitations.
Ultrasound reveals the wall's thinness,
infrared cameras monitor temperature.
Ultraviolet rays identify minerals
in Renaissance pigment.

The face of Christ is now a mask,
the disciples' cries have become muffled.
Every day for months she examines
pinhead patches magnified forty times,
applying solvents, blotting quickly before acid
bites into the most important dying thing
in the world.

An area the size of a postage stamp
takes a week: the tension, exhaustion
build up; so many eyes watching her,
waiting for the emergence of Leonardo
from the slow drip of the centuries.
Some nights she does not sleep:
only the distant drone of a jet engine
can close those eyes.